88

minutes *or less:* Achieving Workplace Success

Steven Blanco

Edited by Marjorie Beatty

Published by
Proactive Training Solutions, Inc.

Arlington, Texas

88 minutes *or less:* Achieving Workplace Success
by Steven Blanco

Published by:
Proactive Training Solutions, Inc.
5904 S. Cooper, Suite 104
Arlington, TX 76017
www.getproactive.com

Unattributed quotations are by Steven Blanco

ISBN 0-9760550-0-7

Library of Congress Control Number 2004111385

For information, inquiries and special prices for bulk quantities, please contact our sales department at 817-465-5800. Contact the author directly at stevenblanco@stevenblanco.com

Printed in the United States of America by PS Media Group, LLC.

About the Author

Steven Blanco's experience in the workplace spans three decades. He started as an hourly employee and in due course was given some supervisory duties. Steven then graduated from Michigan State University and began his career in management. He was promoted several times and lived in eight states along the way.

Today, Steven uses his practical experience as a known nationwide and international speaker. At time of publication, Steven had delivered approximately 1000 speaking dates in 46 states and 3 countries. Steven's expertise in speaking is centered on the workplace.

As Steven traveled the world, he noticed there were some questions and challenges that many employees had in common. These questions and challenges existed from California to Maine and from Sydney to London. He discovered that no effective resource existed that employees could quickly turn to for expert advice.

He also realized that most employees did not have the time to read a 500-page book on the subject of achieving success in the workplace. The employees he spoke with wanted quick solutions that were based on the real world rather than on some theory. Hence, he wrote this book.

Steven is available for speaking engagements. Please visit www.stevenblanco.com for more information.

Preface--
Why 88 minutes, and other interesting tidbits

This book was created specifically to give employees real world tips, tools, and techniques they can use to increase their likelihood of achieving success in the workplace. It is designed to be fun and easy to read and follow.

It will take about 88 minutes to read this book cover to cover. This is based on the concept that on average people read approximately 250 words per minute. The chapters are designed to be "stand-alone." In other words, you can read the chapters that are most applicable to you first without feeling like you are missing something.

Additionally, if you are about to encounter a tough situation in the workplace, you can read or reread a chapter in 5-12 minutes, depending on the chapter you need. You can also listen to the CD audio version of this book. Since the spoken word is only about 150 wpm, it will take a little longer to listen to the CD than to read the book.

Why 88 minutes? The minutes are analogous to the 88 keys on a piano. When a key is played by itself, it does little to inspire. However, played together, these keys provide a great harmony. If there is harmony in the workplace, you are more likely to achieve success individually. You play a greater role in the overall success of the workplace and your individual success than you may realize. I hope you enjoy reading this book!

Acknowledgements

I would like to thank my wife, parents, sister, and friends for their unwavering support in my journey through the workplace and throughout the creation of this book. I dedicate this book to them.

I am grateful to Mark Stephens. His editorial contributions are much appreciated.

Contents

This is your coworker. This is your coworker upset.
Any questions?

Do most people in the workplace with a "bad attitude" know they have a "bad attitude?" NO!

You are thinking, "How could they not know? It is obvious!"

Chapter 1 Handling Coworkers with an Attitude... in 12 minutes *or less*

Do you work with someone with a "bad attitude?" Are you reading this book just to get away from that person with a "bad attitude" for a while? If so, read on, 'cause we're gonna fix it, believe it or not!

This chapter will explore whether these people have a "bad attitude" or just a style that is different from yours. It will also offer strategies for what to do, what to say, and how to say it!

There are two approaches you can take to this person with a "bad attitude." One is to change your behavior and reaction to the person. The second way is to change the person. Though we'll focus on both, which of the two do you think is more effective and easier?

Are They Difficult or Different?

There are certainly some people in the workplace that have what you can call a "bad attitude." However, many times their attitude (or your perception of it) is just different from yours. Let's take a look at the four different types of coworkers we typically find in the workplace: Movers, Doers, Wooers and Provers. Take note of these types and consider what characteristics are familiar to you and similar to those around you.

Movers

These coworkers tend to be very imaginative and creative. They talk with their hands and are very colorful in their expressions. Movers have a lot of ideas and are usually good at working at several things at the same time. Movers keep very busy and are high-energy. They are typically good brainstormers.

Others can sometimes perceive Movers as unable to finish tasks (though they have many going on at the same time), disorganized (typically evidenced by a messy desk), and unrealistic in the things they think are possible. At times, these characteristics can cause them to be perceived as "con artists" by coworkers!

Doers

These coworkers are easy to spot—they want things done and they want them done NOW! They seem to be impatient and have little time for or interest in the personal lives of their coworkers. These individuals appear to always be in charge (whether they have actual authority or not), are influential over other people and are very determined to get what they want.

Others in the workplace might see them as bossy, hardheaded, inflexible dictators who only care about themselves! They might yell, attempt to bully others, and have absolutely no tolerance for coworkers who waste their time.

Wooers

These coworkers are very friendly, and pleasing others is a primary objective for them. These individuals tend to be good listeners, truly care about other people and are sympathetic to their concerns. Others see these people as good team players. In a nutshell, Wooers have excellent people skills and value relationships with others. They really want to be liked.

Others in the workplace may perceive Wooers as overly friendly (sometimes even as fake). They typically do not want to "rock the boat" and often do not speak up for themselves. As a result, some people may take advantage of the Wooers. Others may view them as too interested in the personal affairs of others.

Provers

"Prove it to me" is the common statement heard from these people. They tend to be very organized, methodical and meticulous in their work, and are analytical in nature. They tend to look at a problem from every possible angle before making any type of decision. They are also very detailed, and rely on facts rather than emotions to make decisions at work.

In terms of perceptions, Provers are not seen by others as being very enthusiastic, exciting or "people persons." They tend to be compulsively neat, as well as slow and obsessive in making decisions, and sometimes these individuals are even called "nitpicky." They have a certain process that they go through to make most decisions and this process is largely inflexible.

Strategies

First, decide which one of these coworkers describes you most of the time. Chances are you will not have ALL the characteristics of a certain type of coworker, and you may even exemplify characteristics of some or all of the other types. In some situations in the world, we would say that you have "multiple personalities!" No problem here, however. Next, decide on the type of coworker you view as difficult.

None of these four coworker types is any "better" or "worse" than another as they all have advantages and disadvantages. What follows are the strategies to deal with each type of coworker. Think about it this way: Is it more effective to deal with coworkers the way you would want to be treated or the way they would want to be treated?

It is *easier* (and much more common) to treat them the way you want to be treated, but it is *more effective* to treat them the way they want to be treated!

<u>Movers</u>

One effective strategy to communicate with Movers is to increase your level of enthusiasm and use your hands and arms more expressively. This is particularly challenging for Provers (who prefer to communicate with less enthusiasm and expression), so Provers have to work at it a bit more. Movers also communicate at a fast pace, so be prepared to keep up.

Movers also have a lot of ideas, many of which do not actually work! However, make sure you compliment them on the ideas they did come up with before you systematically tear those ideas to shreds! Movers are proud of their creativity.

Movers are also proud of their multitasking and typically can be found with a messy desk. They will tell you, "My desk IS messy, but I know right where everything is!" And, they usually do! Therefore, try to avoid criticizing their apparent lack of organization.

Another good strategy is to ask Movers lots of questions. Most Movers love answering all kinds of questions (whether they actually know the answer or not). Open-ended questions give Movers an opportunity to show their creativity and are usually more effective than closed-ended questions. For example, ask Movers, "What do you think about the project deadline?" (open-ended) rather than, "Do you think the project will finish on time?" (closed-ended).

<u>Doers</u>

The qualities of a Doer offer a straightforward strategy. However, this strategy may be the hardest to actually implement.

Be direct.

That's it!

Avoid beating around the bush. Get to the point and move on. They are not usually interested in hearing about your personal relationships and often are not concerned with how your day is going. Wooers will have a big problem here! Consider the following conversation between Dave (Doer) and Wendy (Wooer):

(Wendy walks into Dave's office)

Wendy: "Hi, Dave. How are you doing today?"

Dave: "Fine."

Wendy: "Uh, so did you have a good weekend?"

Dave: "OK."

Wendy: "Well, I had a GREAT weekend. My son, Pete, won his soccer match 4-3 and even scored a goal. My daughter, Jane, well she started ballet classes for the first time ever. I think she's gonna do real..."

Dave (interrupting): "Wendy, do you need something?"

Wendy (perceiving Dave to be incredibly rude): "Uh, yeah, I need the ABC Report from this weekend."

Dave: "Here you go. Have a good one."

(Wendy exits).

Wendy thinks Dave has a "bad attitude," right? Does he? Or, is his communication style in the workplace just different?

The next time Wendy is in this position, she could walk into Dave's office and say, "Hi, Dave. I need the ABC Report from this weekend please."

Wendy may even see Dave warming up to her at some point because he appreciates that she is treating him the way he prefers to be treated! Note the suggested strategy does not give us permission to be rude in return. Rather, the strategy requires us to be brief and to the point.

In fact, for the Doers reading this book, you probably thought the above example was unnecessary—right after the suggestion to "be direct," the book could move on to the next type of coworker, right?

Not quite yet. One more point. The way coworkers typically react to Doers in the workplace is to become passive and do whatever the Doers say. Avoid this! Do not become aggressive (in your face) either because aggressive behavior will lead to escalation of the situation and a potential argument. Instead, assert yourself by recognizing that you have rights, and so does the Doer. Not only will this strategy be more effective, the Doer will appreciate it more and have greater respect for you.

A review of Dave's situation in regard to the ABC Report gives us an opportunity to consider three different ways Wendy might react to Dave. This example starts out with Wendy entering Dave's office and saying, "Hi, Dave. I need the ABC Report, please." Dave's response is, "Can't you see I'm busy?"

Wendy's passive response: "Oh, OK. Sorry." Wendy walks out without the report she needs.

Wendy's aggressive response: "Yeah, I'm busy too and I want that report NOW." Situation likely escalates from here!

Wendy's assertive response: "I know you are busy and if I can get the report from you I can get out of your way." In this scenario, Wendy asserts that Dave's time is valuable and she needs the report. She also quickly provides Dave with a benefit of giving her the report now. This strategy is the most likely to be successful.

Doers are often perceived as having a "bad attitude." The fact is, most Doers have a different way of functioning in the workplace.

Wooers

Since Wooers are very friendly, considerate people, the best way to approach them in a work environment is to be friendly in return. Take an honest interest in their personal lives. For example, ask about their kids and how their day is going. This is going to be the hardest for Doers. Remember, the most effective way to be successful is to conform to their desires, not vice-versa.

Wooers value people over ideas. The more they trust you, the more likely they are to get along with you at work. Here's an example:

A Wooer, Wilma, is walking in a park. A stranger comes up to her and says, "If you give me 20 bucks right now, I'll meet you back at this spot tomorrow and magically turn your 20 bucks into $1,000!" There is probably not a Wooer in the world who would do this because it sounds like a crazy idea and no relationship exists between the stranger and Wilma.

In the next scenario, Wilma is walking in the park and her best friend of 30 years, Walter, approaches her and says, "If you give me 20 bucks right now, I'll meet you back at this spot tomorrow and magically turn your 20 bucks into $1,000!" Same crazy idea, right? However, this time there

is a relationship involved. Since W
people, not ideas, most Wooers in Wiln
would fork over the $20. Now, if Wa
come through, the trust level in the ....uonship
has been damaged. Keep that in mind!

Additionally, most Wooers hate conflict of any
kind. They want things to go smoothly. So, if
there is a conflict situation at work, try to get it
resolved quickly, and don't expect the Wooer to
play a key role in fixing the situation.

Provers

Provers have a very methodical and deliberate way
of making decisions. To others, a Prover's system
is painstakingly slow and very detailed. This can
cause frustration for other types of coworkers,
especially Movers. Movers make very quick,
impulsive decisions that usually do not involve
any kind of system at all.

For example, have you ever tried to purchase a
new car with a Prover? The Prover will do hours of
research before buying to ensure s/he gets the
best deal. Some things that will probably be
important to Provers are gas mileage, reliability,
Consumer Reports (or similar) analysis,
depreciation, which colors or vehicle types cost
less money for insurance, resale value, etc.

The Mover, on the other hand, runs into the first
place s/he sees, notices a car on the showroom
floor, and says, "I like the cool red one. I'LL BUY
IT!"

here is a tendency for others to try to rush the Prover through his/her methodical decision-making process and say, "Come on. Let's get the red one!"

Avoid doing this!

The Prover is not going to change how the Prover makes decisions! Therefore, a successful method a person may use to work with a Prover is to show the Prover that what you want fits his/her structure! Explain that the "cool red one" gets good gas mileage, is reliable, and has good resale value.

In the workplace, we tend to view Provers as difficult because of this long process they go through in making a decision. This is the way Provers are—not difficult, but different.

Also, limit your enthusiasm when speaking to a Prover. Slow down and use gestures sparingly to better communicate with these folks. Patience will pay off here!

A Final Thought

Coworkers who are at the centers of most conflicts are the ones with the "v's"—Movers and Provers, and the ones without the "v's"—Doers and Wooers. These pairs will have to work harder in the workplace to get along because they are polar opposites.

Thankfully, we tend to see a mix of all four in the workplace. Imagine an organization with only Movers—nothing would ever get done. Or, if the workplace was filled with only Doers—too many cooks spoil the broth. Or, if the workplace was filled with only Wooers—personal relationships would take precedence over getting the job done. Or, if the workplace was filled with only Provers—decisions would take forever! Obviously, these are exaggerations but you can begin to see the value of having a diverse workplace. It's a plus, not a minus!

Difficult, Not Just Different

The rest of this chapter is dedicated to the truly difficult people we work with and some of the strategies you can use that have proven to be effective.

1. Don't Fuel the Fire!

Remember the "class clown" in high school? What was this person (typically) seeking? ATTENTION! When that person received the attention from teachers, principals and classmates, what did s/he do? The person would keep doing it at an even more intense level.

Sometimes, those with a "bad attitude" in the workplace are looking for attention. We fuel the fire by giving them the attention they seek! In other words, we become enablers. You can try ignoring the problem and see if it goes away.

On the other hand, it may be more effective to find a more productive way to give this person some attention through praise, for example. As long as s/he is getting attention, s/he is happy—so, take control of the situation.

    2. Explain the IMPACT

Here's an interesting question. Do most people in the workplace with a "bad attitude" know they have a "bad attitude?" NO!

You are thinking, "How could they not know? It is obvious!" What may be obvious to you often is not so obvious to this person. For example, do people with bad breath know that they have bad breath? NO! How could they not know? It is obvious! First, they live with it and are used to it. Second, it is likely no one has ever said anything to them about it—at least not in an effective way (see Chapter 8).

Do these people impact the workplace in a negative way? YES! Then, it is important to show them HOW their behavior or performance is affecting you and the team in terms of morale, productivity, quality, quantity, customer service, etc.

For example, let's say your coworker when greeted in the morning responds with a nod and a grunt. Next time that happens, try saying, "When I greet you in the morning and you respond as you just did with a nod and a grunt it puts me in a bad mood and lowers my morale. That's why I avoid you at lunch. I would appreciate it if you would at least look at me and say 'hello.' What do you think?" Most of the time the person will say, "I'm not a morning person and I didn't even realize I was doing that. I apologize, and I'll try to do better in the future." Of course, you won't always get this response, but it is the most likely.

3. Avoid using terms like "bad attitude"

If 100 employees were asked to write a one-sentence definition of "bad attitude" we would probably have 90 different definitions of it!

So, when you tell someone s/he has a "bad attitude," s/he is typically picturing something different than you are! Many times, since the term is so vague, this label *causes* the other person to have a "bad attitude." *You think I have a bad attitude today, wait 'til you see me tomorrow—I'll show you a bad attitude!*

4. Focus on observed behaviors, not inferences

Let's say your coworker, Robby, has lost an important document. He is throwing papers around, yelling, asking you if you did something with his document, and then he asks if he can search your desk. The way someone would tell Robby (later) about what happened in the workplace probably goes something like this:

"You were acting like a madman because you lost a document. You were REALLY irritated and even accused me of stealing it. You became so furious that you were about ready to punch a hole in the wall. You got all stressed out and gave me a bad attitude about it as well."

Everything in the above example represents your *inferences* or perceptions about the event, rather than *facts* about what happened. How do you know he was irritated, furious, stressed out and was ready to punch a hole in the wall? You don't, because you are not inside his head! What you DO know about are the observed behaviors. In other words, ask yourself, "Could I take a picture of it?" Could you take a picture of him throwing papers around and yelling? YES. Convey the facts to Robby. *Then* you might say, "Since you were yelling so loud, it looked like you were going to punch a hole in the wall."

Use the standard "Can I take a picture of it?" Convey *that* to the person with a "bad attitude."

No matter which technique you use, remember that you have a lot more control over your coworker's "bad attitude" than you may realize. You can always control your approach and reaction to that person.

"Yes, sir...I understand you are upset...yes, I know you are the customer...well, um, suppose we refund your money, give you our product free for life, send you on a trip to the Bahamas and physically torture every employee who has ever made our product. Would *that* satisfy you???"

As a note, most challenging customers do not want or need to talk to a manager. In fact, most challenging customers prefer to have their complaint resolved by the person who initially addressed their situation.

Chapter 2
Dealing With Challenging Customers...in 12 minutes *or less*

Your job would be so much easier if it weren't for those darn customers getting in the way of everything! They complain. They demand. They are rude. They want everything now at a lower cost with a higher quality. And, if it weren't for "those people," you would be able to stay at home and read this book since you would not have a job. Assuming you could still afford your home, that is!

If you have a job, then you have a customer. This customer may be internal or external, but you have a customer—someone who relies on a

product or service that you provide.   In return,
you receive a paycheck.

This chapter gives you insight into why customers
act the way they do and what actions you can
take to successfully deal with the customer.   By
the way, the customer is not always right, but the
customer is always the customer.   Sometimes,
however, the mistake is our own fault.   Here is a
personal example:

> At one point in my career, I was
> working in upper management at a
> large hotel in the Chicago area.   The
> hotel was hosting a big convention for
> the   Illinois   Department   of
> Transportation (IDOT). We had a large
> sign in the parking lot in front of the
> hotel that would be changed nightly to
> welcome a special group by name. Nice
> personal touch.   I was working that
> evening, so when I pulled up to the
> hotel for work, the attendees of the
> convention had already arrived.
>
> You can imagine the shock and horror I
> felt when I read the sign on my way in:
>
> W E L C O M E
>
>
> I D I O T S
>
> OK—so, the employees we had putting
> up the sign could not spell so well.
>
> OOPS!

> If anyone from IDOT is reading this book,
> I *continue* to offer my apologies, more
> than a decade later!

Sometimes, things are going to go wrong. What counts is how you handle the problems that come your way.

Shedding "Shoulds"

This is an important component of effectively dealing with customers!

Suppose you are driving in the right hand lane of a two-lane highway with both lanes heading in the same direction. There is another car, "Car X" that has been in the left hand lane beside you for the last ½ mile. You do not know the person in Car X.

Up ahead, you see a road sign indicating that the lane Car X is driving in is about to end. There are also orange cones ahead indicating the same thing.

In this scenario, what *should* Car X do? Avoid focusing on what you will do. What *should* Car X do? Check one of the boxes below:

☐   Car X *should* speed up and get ahead of me

☐   Car X *should* slow down and yield behind me

Now, we're going to switch cars. YOU are in the left hand lane and your lane is ending. Car X is in

the right hand lane. Given the exact same
scenario, what *will* YOU do?

☐ I will speed up and get ahead of Car X

☐ I will slow down and yield behind Car X

Most people think that Car X in the left hand lane
should slow down and yield. However, most
people will say that if *they* were in the left hand
lane, they would speed up and get ahead!

So, when the car in the left hand lane speeds up
to get ahead, what does the car in the right hand
lane do? That's right—the car speeds up because
the driver feels that the car in the left hand lane
should yield!

Can you see now why we have road rage?

So, who is right? Who *should* get in front?

Your perspective is the key, isn't it?

What does the law say in this situation? Well, in
most states (if not all), the law says the car in the
left hand lane is supposed to yield to the car in
the right lane! So, those of you who chose to
speed up when you were driving Car X are
breaking the law (quick—change your answer
before a police officer sees it)!

Consider another example. You are at the grocery
store, and you are in a hurry. You have filled
your cart, and are fifth in line. The person

directly in front of you is going to pay for his/her groceries by writing a check. The question for you is:

Should the person writing a check begin to fill out the parts of the check already known (name of store, date, check register information, signature, etc.) *before* s/he arrives to the cashier?

☐   Yes, s/he *should*

☐   No, s/he *should not*

☐   Even though I am in a hurry, I do not care

Most of you probably selected the first box. What made you choose the first box? Your responses might include:

"It's common courtesy"

"S/he *should* respect the time of others"

"S/he is not doing anything else, anyway"

"It is common sense"

"That's what I would do if I were her/him"

The question raised is, "who is right?"

What does the law say about this? Courtesy in a grocery store line has not been addressed, at least not yet. However, if you ask most law enforcement professionals, they would likely advise someone not to get out their checkbook and fill it out until in front of the cashier!

What is the grocery store policy? There is no policy! Perhaps the person who is paying with a check thinks the store register automatically prints all the information on the check, as some places do.

Again, who is right?

Everybody!

What we often do is to project how we would handle a situation onto someone else. When that person does not do what you think s/he *should* do in a given situation, you are offended and believe the person lacks "common sense." Whose version of "common sense?" *Yours!*

Consider a final example. You are at the grocery store, still in a hurry, and you enter the "10 Items or Less" Express Lane. The person in front of you already has the following items in the cart:

- 20 boxes of Frosted Flakes cereal
- 10 Snickers candy bars
- 20 cans of Alpo dog food

Question: How many "Items" does s/he have?

☐ 50 Items

☐ 3 Items

Most of you checked the first box, and felt very strongly about it! Well, there are definitely 50 pieces in the cart. The question is, what is an "item?"

What is the law? There isn't one.

What is the grocery store policy? There isn't one! The grocery store does not define an "item."

People who would claim there are three items might point out that the cashier needs only to scan one box, then hit "X 20". Yeah, but the items still need to get bagged. The debate could go on forever!

Plus, who knows what happened before you got in line. Maybe this cashier was not busy, and called this customer over from another lane that was not an Express Lane. We just do not know.

However, does the Express Lane situation violate your sense of what someone *should* or *should not* do? Who is right? You believe that you are, and it greatly affects your perception of the person.

Customers are the same way. When a customer acts differently than we think s/he *should* act, it violates our sense of right and wrong. Remember, we also do not have an idea what may have happened to that customer before s/he came in contact with us. In the earlier driving example, the person in Car X may have had a family emergency. We would not know this but, if we somehow may have learned this, would it make it OK for Car X to get ahead of you? Probably.

So, *shed your shoulds*, and let's get on with how to deal with these customers.

The Five Steps

Have you noticed how poor customer service is in some places? Better yet, have you observed how poorly things are handled when something does go wrong?

Listed below are five easy steps you can take when something goes wrong and you encounter that challenging customer. Implementing these steps into your daily work life will create happier, more satisfied customers. If your customers are happier, you will be, too.

Step One: Listen and Record

The truth is that most of us are not very good listeners. We tend to listen to respond, instead of to understand. When someone is talking and you find yourself formulating your response to the question or statement while the other person is talking, it is highly likely that you are not listening. If you are interrupting the other person, s/he will automatically assume (right or wrong) that you are not listening.

If you fail to maintain at least periodic eye contact with the person (or fail to use short verbal agreements on the telephone), s/he will assume you are not listening.

Please remember most of us have the capacity to listen to more than three times as many words as the average person can speak. Therefore, it is only natural to have our minds wander off from the conversation at hand.

So, to be successful, discipline yourself to really tune in. Try to limit distractions, such as papers on your desk, ringing cell phones and other interruptions. Focus on what the customer is saying. Many times, you can learn a lot simply by listening.

Additionally, write down what the customer is telling you. This sends a strong statement to the customer that you are going to seriously act upon the complaint, suggestion, etc. If you are on the telephone, let the customer know that you will be taking notes. Recording also helps ensure you get all the details. These notes will be important to have for the remaining steps.

Step Two: Paraphrase and Empathize

Paraphrase simply means to put what the customer said into your own words in a brief manner. It really lets the customer know that you have been listening, and will help ensure good communication. On the other hand, miscommunication may cause the problem to become more serious.

Here is an example of a customer complaint, followed by an appropriate response:

Customer: "I was told by three people in your office that the delivery would be made to me today by noon. They all promised me it would not be late again. Well, I guess they lied. Now, I have to explain to my customer that his order will not be ready when I promised him because of your company's mistake. I ought to have this customer call you directly so you can deal with his wrath!"

You: "So, we promised you a delivery time and now your customer is going to be affected. Is that correct?"

Next, empathize. What ever happened to the art of empathy?

Have you ever flown on a commercial airline when the plane did not land at the time you were told it was going to land? Did the airline personnel empathize in any way, or did you get the feeling they just did not care. After all, the delay was affecting you, not them.

Empathy is different from sympathy. Sympathy is to feel sorry for someone. Empathy is to put yourself in that person's shoes and understand how s/he must feel. There are three levels of empathy. It is important to select the right level so that you are credible to your customer. To explain these levels, let's say you are talking to a coworker who has just had a manager turn down his/her vacation request.

Level One: You have experienced the exact same thing, and completely understand the other person's position. You might say, "I experienced the same thing myself, and I know how you feel."

Level Two: You've had a day off request turned down before, but it was not a vacation request. So, you experienced something similar. You could say, "I had a request for a day off rejected, and that day was very important to me. Though it was not as bad as an entire vacation being turned down, I can understand how you feel."

Level Three: You have never experienced this before, or anything similar. You could say, "I have never personally experienced anything like that, but I can certainly imagine how disappointing it must be."

Bear in mind that empathy is important, but it must be genuine!

Step Three: Apologize, and Find Out What Will Satisfy Him/Her

How many times in your life have you felt someone wronged you, and all you needed to hear was, "I'm sorry?" A sincere apology can go a long way towards soothing these challenging customers.

To find out what will satisfy the customer, consider this example:

You and your significant other, Pat, are eating at a nice restaurant to celebrate Pat's birthday. You are drinking a bottle of wine, and have already eaten some appetizers, which were very good. Your entrée arrives, and it is very good. Pat is enjoying the fish s/he ordered until s/he eats a piece from the middle that is cold. A short time later, Pat says s/he feels ill and runs to the restroom. The manager walks over to your table while Pat is in the restroom. What would the manager need to say or do at this point to *personally* satisfy you in this situation?

Think about it, and then check any/all of the following that would apply:

_____Apologize
_____Find out if Pat is OK
_____Go to the kitchen and find out why the fish
        was cold in the middle
_____Get Pat another fish
_____Get Pat a different entrée of his/her choice
_____No charge for Pat's entrée
_____Free dessert
_____No charge for the bottle of wine
_____No charge for the appetizers
_____The entire meal is free
_____Give you and Pat a gift certificate to return
        again "on the house"
_____The entire meal is free, plus the gift
        certificate is provided for next time.

The list above is the entire range of possibilities a large group of people would give if presented with this exact same scenario. Note that you see everything from only an apology to a free dinner this time and next time the patrons dine in the restaurant.

Therefore, it is important to realize that solutions to problems and to challenging customers must be customized, rather than resolved through a "cookie cutter" approach. For example, the manager may have come over and apologized and paid for the entire meal. However, if all you wanted was for the manager to check on Pat and see if s/he is OK, then the manager's solution will not satisfy you!

As a note, most challenging customers do not want or need to talk to a manager. In fact, most challenging customers prefer to have their complaint resolved by the person who initially addressed their situation. Your ability to do this will vary based on company policy, your manager's philosophy and your own personal comfort level on how to handle the issue.

Step Four: Propose a Solution, then Get Approval

By this point, you will know what would satisfy the customer by listening carefully (step one) and paraphrasing (step two). You have also built trust with the customer through recording (step one), empathizing (step two) and apologizing (step three). Now, you will feel confident to propose a solution, *and then* get approval from the customer.

In the restaurant example above, propose a solution and then get approval from the customer: "I will not charge you for Pat's dinner, and I will let him/her pick another entrée from the menu." (Pause) "Does that sound fair to you?"

This is strong. An example of a weak statement would be, "Well, would it be OK if we just paid for Pat's dinner?"

If the customer says "No," then you'll need to back up to steps three, two or one. Unless a "last resort" option is needed, it is generally not advisable to ask, "What can we do to make this right?" Remember, you are the expert here, and you know what you can offer to make it right.

Step Five: Follow Up

The final step is a key component to achieving success in dealing with challenging customers. One part of the follow-up is with the customer to make sure that whatever solution you proposed went smoothly.

The other part of follow-up requires your coworkers, boss and other pertinent company officials to dig down deep, find the root of the problem, and fix it in order to prevent the problem from occurring again. The most effective way to deal with challenging customers is to minimize the likelihood they will have a reason to become challenging in the first place!

Significantly, most studies show that only a small number of dissatisfied customers ever complain. They usually just stop using your company's products or services and they often tell at least 10 people about their bad experience.

One More Challenging Customer

People are always asking for advice on how to handle an irate customer. If you follow the guidelines set forth in the chapter (shed your *shoulds*, and follow the Five Steps), most irate customers will calm down. But, what if they don't?

Keep in mind that the irate customer is probably not angry with you. S/he is angry at the situation. So, do not take what the irate customer is saying personally.

Even if it was your fault, no one deserves to receive treatment such as screaming, or other disrespectful behavior. A passive approach here will just cause the customer to continue, and an aggressive response will only make matters worse. If you've done everything in this chapter, and the customer is still irate, try this:

"Sir/Ma'm, I can definitely help you with this, and I can only help you if you are willing to treat me as a person--with dignity and respect." You will be surprised how many people are disarmed by this simple statement, sometimes to the point of offering you an apology for their actions!

Above all else, remember that paycheck you receive? The customer is the one who writes it.

"Now, Bert, as your boss I feel like you need to come up with more creative ideas in your job. Currently, if I gave you a penny for your thoughts I'd get change back."

While your manager is delivering your review, you may have a strong urge to flip to the last page to see the "score." Try to avoid doing this. Rather, listen intently to what the manager is saying. Ask questions to clarify. Assertively communicate whenever you disagree with part of the evaluation.

Chapter 3 Receiving a Better Performance Review... in 5 minutes *or less*

Companies and organizations typically review their employees on a formal basis once or twice a year, or more. Since there are no real regulations regarding performance reviews, the timing, the content, the length, the frequency, the reviewer and whether or not a merit increase is included are completely at the discretion of the employer.

Since these reviews are often used to determine significant areas such as raises, promotions, demotions, job transfer requests, etc., this chapter will focus on understanding these performance reviews from an employer's perspective and helping you maximize your review.

The Manager's Viewpoint

"Would you rather conduct a performance review or have all your teeth pulled out without Novocain?"

If you asked a group of managers this question, you would be shocked to see the number of managers who would choose to be toothless!

The majority of managers do not like conducting appraisals because reviews tend to be confrontational. Uh, make that, YOU tend to be confrontational! You do this with good reason, however. Many times, the manager is sharing new information with you that has not been shared before. Yet, this new information is now part of your permanent record.

Isn't this the *manager's* problem? No, it quickly becomes *your* problem. Here are some things you can do to help lessen the possibility this will happen to you:

  1. Get copies of your prior review(s)

In many states, employers are legally obligated to show you what is in your personnel file. In several states, they are required to give you copies of your file on request (they usually charge you for the copies at cost). Even in states where employers are not legally required to show you prior reviews, companies usually will if you ask them.

Look at these reviews and note the identified areas for improvement (whether you agree with them or not is not the issue at this point; they are in your file).

Then, set goals to improve the areas of weakness (see Chapter 10 for more information). Consult with your manager when setting the goals, and ask for a formal periodic follow-up (such as monthly or quarterly) on those goals.

   2. Talk to your manager

Have informal conversations from time to time and ask how you are doing. Specifically ask if there is anything s/he thinks you need to work on before your performance review is due.

   3. Clearly understand all facets of the review

What are the categories? How are you being measured? Are you measured against a standard or against your coworkers? If you are new to the organization or the position, ask for a copy of a blank review so you will have an idea of the criteria on which you will be evaluated.

All Feedback is Good Feedback!

One of the characteristics of a good evaluation is the delivery of feedback in a constructive manner. Unfortunately, it doesn't always happen that way.

In fact, here are some comments that have reportedly been written on reviews in the past:

"This employee should go far...and the sooner he does, the better."

"This employee would argue with a sign post."

"Gate is down, lights are flashing, but the train isn't coming."

"This employee has a full six-pack, but lacks the little plastic thing to hold it all together."

Ouch! Those are tough to take, but there is probably a message behind each of them despite the poor way they were stated.

Here is a personal story about receiving feedback.

> To set the stage, I've learned from my experiences in approximately 1,000 live speaking engagements in 46 states and three countries that feedback is vital. Therefore, I make every effort to gather written feedback via evaluation form after every speaking engagement.

> On this occasion, I had just presented for about 200 people. When I got the evaluations back, 199 of the reviews were extremely positive about my presentation. However, one participant was not so thrilled. She said that she did not like my presentation because she did not feel like I made personal eye contact with her

as the lights above reflected in my glasses. Instead of seeing my eyes, she saw lights.

Now, I did not initially take this criticism in the constructive manner in which I am sure it was intended. After all, I have puttingthingsinmyeye-aphobia (look it up) and was not about to start wearing contact lenses! However, I did "store" the feedback for future validation.

About a year later, my wife decided it was time for me to get new glasses. She believes that new glasses are necessary every so often to, you know, stay "in style" as a professional speaker. If it was not for her, I very well might be wearing glasses that were in style in the '70's.

So, off we went to purchase new glasses for me. Now, the way this process works is that I go sit in a chair while my wife and the sales associate pick out my new frames. When do you think they summon me? That's right, *when it is time to pay for the glasses!*

I sat down with the sales associate, and she said, "Mr. Blanco, what type of lenses do you want?"

"Uh, " I replied, "What are my choices?"

She proceeded to list a number of different types of lenses (whatever happened to good ol' glass?) until one caught my attention.

"...anti-glare..."

"Whoa! What did you say?"

She repeated the choice, and then proceeded to explain: "You know, when other people look at you and all they see are lights, or you look at a streetlight at night and it looks like a fireworks display on the Fourth of July?"

Pause.

"I'LL TAKE THOSE!" I blurted out as the memory of the stored feedback flashed through my head.

"Well," she said, "They are very expensive and you have to take really good care of them. If they are dirty, you can't just rub them on your tie or with your finger."

"SOUNDS GREAT—I'LL TAKE THEM!"

And so, the glasses I wear today are a result of seemingly useless feedback I received. Others likely had the same reaction to my glasses too, over the years, but nobody ever said anything to me, probably because they thought there was nothing I could do about it anyway.

So, bear in mind that all feedback is good feedback!

When You Get Your Review

While your manager is delivering your review, you may have a strong urge to flip to the last page to see the "score." Try to avoid doing this. Rather, listen intently to what the manager is saying. Ask questions to clarify. Assertively communicate whenever you disagree with part of the evaluation.

Finally, take advantage of whatever your organization offers to voice your feelings about the review. This includes writing something under the "employee comments" section and using the open door policy. Wait a day before you do either, just to make sure you have everything in perspective.

Remember—your review is part of your permanent personnel record and you need to be as proactive as possible in affecting its outcome.

Evaluation Exercise

Obtain a blank copy of your performance review. Complete it (do a self-appraisal). Ask for a meeting with your manager and explain that you are striving to get a better review the next time, and you need his/her help. Talk about the review you just gave yourself, and ask the manager for points of agreement or disagreement.

Today's date:

Date for completion:

"OK, boss...so, as you can see here, we have the sales I have produced over the past several years. Now, er, if we flip this same graph on its left side, we can, um, see my salary history over the same time period."

To be successful, the employee must take his/her emotions out of the process. No reason exists for the company to give you a raise simply because you "really need the extra money."

Chapter 4
Getting a
Promotion or
Raise...in 7
minutes *or less*

How many of you started reading this book right here, rather than with chapter one?

Truth be told, one of the best ways to get a promotion or raise is to read this book and start implementing some of the strategies. In other words, this chapter should probably be last. But it isn't. We want answers, and we want them quickly—in seven minutes or less, to be precise. So, let's go...

Many people feel they should get a promotion or raise because "The company OWES me!"

Let's set the record straight. First of all, the only thing the company "owes" an employee is a paycheck that at least covers your state's minimum wage laws. That's pretty much it. If you are waiting around for that promotion or raise because of a belief of entitlement, you may be waiting a very, very long time.

The employee has to be proactive, must go out and strive to get it. Instead of waiting for your ship to come in, go ahead and swim out to it. What follows are the "swimming" lessons.

Getting a Promotion

Many employees often overlook the most effective way to get a promotion. You know you want that promotion. You want it bad. Your family knows it. Your friends know it. Your boss knows it, and your coworkers are tired of hearing about it!

Everyone knows it.

Everyone except the person or people making the actual decision!

Make sure the people who actually make the call on a promotion know your specific intentions. Get a job description (if one exists) to fully understand the expectations of the job. Any employee who wants a promotion must be certain of the company's qualifications and expectations necessary to excel in the job.

When you feel these qualifications have been met or exceeded, the decision-maker should be aware of HOW each of the criteria has been achieved or surpassed. If you fall short in one or more areas, don't give up. Set some concrete goals to achieve these qualifications (see chapter 10 for more details). Some organizations may even make exceptions if they see the employee is working hard with a game plan in place to meet the qualifications (getting a college degree, for example).

It may also be helpful to talk to the person currently holding the position you want. This depends on the person, of course. Find out as much about this job as possible from this person, and learn what it took for this person to get the job. Help this person in the desired position to move up. Making him/her look good makes you look good.

One of the best ways to get promoted is to have some potential replacements available for your job. Take an interest in showing someone else how to do your job. Many employees feel threatened and think, "If I am the only one who knows how to do this job, then that is my job security."

The reality is that we are *all* replaceable and the organization would go on surviving tomorrow, even without us. If a list of potential replacements are available to give to the company, that doesn't usually make you replaceable. It makes you promotable!

Once the employee is placed in a position to get promoted, a stronger likelihood exists that an interview will take place. Many employees unfortunately underestimate this part of the process. They think, "This is just a formality. The company already knows who I am."

This is a mistake. Look at this interview as a competition. You are probably up against both internal and external candidates. Accordingly, a big part of getting the job will depend on how your interviewing skills stack up against the other candidates.

Make sure you are well prepared. Research the position. Dress for the part you hope to get. Have a list of questions ready to ask company officials about the job (if you are given the opportunity). Be ready to prove why you are the best candidate for the job.

Here is something you can and should do to prepare for the job. Take a look at the job description and pick out five things that are important elements of the job. Then, think about what you have done in your current job (the more specific the better) that demonstrates you are already capable of assuming the new position. Make note of the specific contribution and place it next to the item on the job description. Now, you are prepared to show the company that you are qualified for the job.

If you've made some mistakes in your current job, be ready to show how those mistakes became learning opportunities that will help you in your future position.

Above all, be honest. Realize that you are selling yourself to the company. Many employees think, "I will be a productive employee when I get that promotion." Unfortunately, it does not work that way. Companies tend to promote people who are already doing well in their current job and show capability of moving to the next step.

After the interview, write a quick thank you note to the interviewer(s) just as you would if you were an external candidate. If you do not get the promotion, don't retreat into a black hole of bitterness. Pick yourself up, dust yourself off, and figure out what goals you need to set to achieve success next time. Most likely, the company will be observing you more closely over the next several weeks to see how you handle the setback. Show them you are a professional, and increase your chances of getting the promotion the next time it becomes available. At the very least, the company will know you are assertive.

Getting a Raise

It is important to understand that requesting a raise is a negotiation between you and the employer, and it needs to be treated that way. In any negotiation, the best way to get what you want is to help the other side (your employer, in this case) get what they want.

To be successful, the employee must take his/her emotions out of the process. Remember, the company does not "owe" you a raise! Also, no reason exists for the company to give you a raise simply because you "really need the extra money."

So, as with any successful negotiation, start with a paradigm. In other words, follow the examples that have been set out previously with other employees to justify a pay raise. Are most people in other companies who perform your same responsibilities making more money?   Most organizations like to pay competitively. In fact, many companies conduct a competitive wage survey at least once a year to make sure they are doing just that.

However, contrary to popular belief, creating the raise paradigm is not enough to actually get a raise. The company wants to know what they will get in return for the extra money they are giving you. The raise has to provide an ROI, or Return on Investment.

In other words, what specifically are you going to do to earn the extra money?

You may be thinking, "I already do enough as it is. They owe it to me." You *are* working hard, and you probably do deserve some more money. But, it doesn't work that way.

Once you have your paradigm and your ROI, do further investigation about the decision-making process.   Who is going to make the ultimate decision? Should you work through your boss, or simply inform him/her about your plan and ask for support? How have raises traditionally been given in the past?

Timing is also very important. Has the company enjoyed good profits over the past three months, or are they struggling? Perhaps they just landed a new account. How long ago did you receive your last pay increase? As with most things, timing is everything!

When the time is right, you are ready. Ask for a meeting and submit your proposal. Do it in writing. Be prepared to show the decision-maker how the requested money will be more than paid for by your future results.

You may also be successful by proposing that you will perform at a higher level over a period of, say, the next 90 days. If you are successful through the proposal period, the company agrees to give you the raise. If not, then they do not.

Other Considerations

Threatening your employer typically does not work! ("Give me a raise or I'll quit!") Remember, this is a negotiation. Idle threats are a one-sided approach. In any successful negotiation, both sides are happy with the process and the outcome. There are cases where some employers will give in to these threats out of necessity. As a result, the employee has "won." *But, what did the employee really "win"?* In many cases, the employee has "won" the employer's resentment because s/he was cornered and threatened.

Always think about preserving the relationship in any negotiation. The goal is to get what you want, make sure the other side is OK with it, and keep the relationship moving in a positive direction.

In another situation, an employee may have an offer from another company and s/he may wish to use this as "leverage" in the negotiation. This may be a part of the negotiation, but should not be the entire premise for the negotiation. Certainly, good employers want to keep their best people. At the same time, the economics of the situation will dictate the outcome most of the time.

Will all your attempts to get a raise be successful? Of course not. However, you have planted the seed so that the next time you might succeed. As with promotions, if your proposal is turned down, it is vital that you keep performing at your current level, or you may jeopardize your ability to get a raise next time around.

If you successfully receive a raise, keep it to yourself! Animosity may be created if you tell a bunch of your coworkers about the raise. Others will want (and truly believe they deserve) a raise. This will cause disruption for the organization—a disruption they are sure to remember the next time YOU ask for a raise!

Bernie the boss always made an extra effort to appear to be open and friendly whenever employees walked in his door.

Several different studies indicate that the number one reason why employees voluntarily quit their jobs is poor communication from their manager. So, if you think your boss is a poor communicator, you are not alone.

Chapter 5 Surviving a Bad Boss...in 11 minutes *or less*

Being a boss is not easy. Sometimes, the pressures involved and the key decisions that must be made are overwhelming. It is not hard to make what appears to be (and what may be) a bad decision. This chapter is not intended to nitpick at every little thing managers do (or do not do). Instead, it is intended to show you real-world ways to cope with the worst of them all: The bad boss.

This chapter is about survival. In other words, what an employee can do to make the experience as pleasant as possible. The chapter is not about changing your boss, because a truly bad boss probably will not change.

There are several different types of bad bosses out there. This chapter will focus on the five that are most commonly found:

1. Two-Faced
2. Tyrant
3. Slave Driver
4. Meek
5. Poor Communicator

Two-Faced

This type of bad boss, let's call him John, is easy to spot. He tells the employee one thing to his/her face, and then tells someone else another thing behind the person's back. John has the potential to ruin your opportunities for advancement and wage increases. He also has the capability to distort your image to the senior-level managers.

There are several traditional, yet generally unsuccessful, ways of dealing with John. If ignored, John will only use these two-faced actions more often. Getting upset and complaining to coworkers might make you feel better but doesn't solve the problem either. In fact, it could make things worse if John finds out you are complaining about him. Responding to John in a sarcastic way or becoming aggressive only fuels him to continue this behavior.

There is a strategy that works much better than those just mentioned. This strategy combines quick documentation with assertiveness, and is called "docusertive."

Here's an example of how "docusertive" works. Let's say that John is having a conversation with you on how he wants you to handle an important customer who is unhappy about the recent service from your company. John encourages you to give the customer a 25% discount. However, you are sure that when John's boss, Keith, finds out about the 25% discount, John will deny any involvement and say you acted alone.

The first part of "docusertive" is to get a verbal commitment from John. At the end of your conversation, you can say, "John, I understand you are in agreement with me to offer the customer the 25% discount. Is that correct?" Wait for a reply, and then continue, "Do I have your commitment that you will support me in the event that Keith disagrees with the decision?"

The next part of "docusertive" is to send John a quick e-mail (or memo if e-mail is not an option). Here is an example:

> Today's Date
>
> John:
>
> Thank you for your guidance and decision to offer the customer a 25% discount. If I have somehow misinterpreted your decision on this, please notify me at once.

In the worse case scenario, Keith disagrees with the decision, calls you and John into his office, and John denies authorizing the 25% discount. In this event, you can remind John about your conversation with him, and show him the e-mail that is sitting on his computer. Do not present this as an "in your face" slam; rather, point out that he "may have forgotten" about your consensual agreement.

Will "docusertive" cause John to change? Perhaps not. However, it will demonstrate to the organization what is really going on (most employers want to know this). This technique will also protect your reputation and increase your chances of surviving this bad boss!

Tyrant

This bad boss is characterized primarily by a dictatorship style. Let's call this person Ty. Ty tends to yell and scream. He is very direct, confrontational, may demean coworkers in front of others, and is driven to achieve results.

Many strategies exist that will not work when the employee attempts to apply them to the situations with Ty. Being passive (ignoring him) will give him the opportunity to think of you as "weak." This weakness is something he will continue to use for his benefit. Becoming aggressive (matching his level) will only cause him to take his aggression to a higher level. This is a no-win situation for anyone. Keep trying these strategies at your own risk!

What does work? Well, for starters, try to be direct with Ty at all times. In other words, do not beat around the bush. If there is a problem in the workplace, do not try to hide it from Ty. Ask for a meeting, be very brief (almost to the point of being "short"), have a couple of solutions to the problem that Ty can choose from, and GET OUT!

This strategy is difficult for those of you who like to develop the relationship and start with "small talk." Ty does not want either of these and will respect you more for communicating with him in the way in which he prefers to be communicated with.

If Ty screams at you in front of others or demeans you, the best way to handle that is the assertive approach. For example, "Ty (or Mr. Ty!), I am willing to take responsibility for the fact that I did turn in the report late *and*, in the future, I would appreciate it if I was spoken to in this manner behind closed doors rather than in front of my coworkers."

By using this strategy, you accept responsibility (which is what Ty wants) and you assert how you want to be treated in the future.

Does this ensure Ty will change? Of course not! However, he may scream less often (at you) and you'll feel better that you stood up for yourself while still respecting his rights. In other words, this strategy will help you survive!

By the way, bosses like Ty are normally "straight shooters" and you usually know where you stand with them. Most employees, therefore, would choose Ty over John any day of the week.

Slave Driver

This bad boss, let's call her Sadie, is characterized by two traits. First, Sadie keeps dumping more and more work on you to the point where you think you are going to explode. Second, she believes that the more hours you work, the better.

In the workplace, most people deal with Sadie by, well, not dealing with Sadie. We tend to go ahead and accept responsibilities that cannot be achieved within the time frame requested. Likewise, we work the long hours it takes to accomplish the tasks (see Chapter 12 for information on achieving balance in and outside the workplace). This approach tends to result in more and more work being piled upon you.

Think about it. For Sadie, it is easier to offload the majority of the work on the person who just accepts it and doesn't say anything, isn't it?

Another common approach is to accept the extra work from Sadie, and complain about it to coworkers, friends and family. When word gets back to Sadie (and it will), she will view you as a complainer, a whiner, and a problematic employee. This perception will only encourage her to give you more work!

By the way, it is important to realize that it is the manager's job to delegate responsibility. Everyone today is expected to do more for less—less cost, less time, and fewer resources—with increased expectations of quality from the end-user (customer). Thus, a bad boss is not one who delegates responsibility. This bad boss dumps an impossible amount of work on you and demands that you work a tremendous amount of hours, whether work exists or not.

There is an effective way to handle Sadie. First, think about the impact of what is going on here. Are all these extra hours and responsibilities beneficial to you? No. You are tired, frustrated, and probably do not have the quality of life that you need to be happy. Are these things benefiting your coworkers? No. They can all see you are tired, frustrated and unhappy. No one likes working around miserable, crabby people. Are these things benefiting the customer? No. Over a period of time, your quality of work will suffer, and the end user will be affected. Is the company benefiting? No. If you are unhappy, you can cause your coworkers to be unhappy, and you can make the customer unhappy as well; all three of these will likely lead to lower productivity, which makes the company unhappy!

Well, *someone* must benefit from this situation.

Is it Sadie?

Not really. If employees and customers are unhappy, and productivity is down, Sadie's job may be at risk. So, when you accept all the extra work and put in a huge amount of hours, all of the parties involved are hurt!

The answer? The next time Sadie comes to you with more work, tell her what you *can* do. (Note: the book did not just say, "Tell her where she can go!")

Here's an example. You begin the day with two reports, A and B. These reports need to be done by the end of the day. Even working at your full capacity, A and B will consume the entire day. Sadie comes up to you at 10am and says, "I need this new report, C, done by the end of the day." The "old you" may have responded, "Uh...I'm really busy...OK." Next time, try this response:

"OK, I can do that. However, reports A and B alone will take the rest of the day to complete. Which report, A or B, would you like me to turn in tomorrow instead of today?"

This strategy gives the boss some control and allows her to prioritize the work. At the same time, it gives you the opportunity to affirm what can be done in the allotted time. Will this strategy work every time? No, she may still say, "Get all three reports done by the end of the day." However, you have planted the seed. Keep in mind that most managers have no idea about your workload and how long it takes to do it properly. Their job is to coordinate the efforts of the entire team. You have to take the step as the "expert" in your area to survive this bad boss.

Meek

This bad boss, Mike, is passive in his approach and avoids any kind of conflict at all costs. He would rather make no decision at all than make a decision that might end up being the wrong one. This behavior causes employee frustration and an overall lack of direction in the workplace.

Faced with this type of boss, most employees simply go along with Mike (because, after all, he *is* the boss). In the worst-case scenario, employees reflect Mike's behavior and are also meek.

The best way to handle Mike is to show him how his actions are affecting the workplace. Once Mike actually sees the impact of his style, he may consider changing his actions.

As an example, one of your coworkers is constantly late to work. Mike doesn't say anything to this person because it might cause a confrontation. So, what's the result? The coworker keeps coming in late and others in the department become angry and resentful.

The solution? Approach Mike and let him know that it appears as though this coworker is late quite often, and nothing is being done about it. Express the frustration that you as well as other team members feel. Explain the conduct's impact on customers, morale, productivity, quality, or any other important company value. Ask for his help. Tell him he is going to have to make a choice between confronting the late coworker (who is breaking company policy and knows it) or confronting the rest of the employees in the department who are angry and trying to do their jobs.

If Mike still does not take any action, set up a meeting with Mike and the other coworkers. He may soon learn that confronting one person who is not performing is much easier to swallow than confronting several employees who are.

Eventually, people will quit because of Mike. When this happens, encourage others to share their reasons for quitting with Mike.

This strategy is not guaranteed to change this bad boss, but it affords you the greatest chance of *surviving* him!

Poor Communicator

Several different studies indicate that the number one reason why employees voluntarily quit their jobs is poor communication from their manager. So, if you think your boss is a poor communicator, you are not alone.

This bad boss, Paula, fails to tell employees about important information and fails to praise or recognize employees in any way for a job well done.

The most common approach employees take here is to, well, communicate. Unfortunately, many people end up communicating with *other coworkers* rather than with Paula. Eventually, however, the grapevine winds its way back to Paula, and the accompanying results can be quite unpleasant for you.

The best approach here is for you to become more proactive in the way you communicate with your boss.

Yeah, but that is HER job.

Keep taking that approach, and you'll keep getting the same miserable results.

OK. So, what do I do?

Let's consider praise and recognition. How would you answer the question, "How many times each week do you receive praise in the workplace?"

OK, stop laughing.

Seriously.

If you said 0-2 times per week, you would be among the norm!

Note that the question *did not* state, "How many times each week do you get praised *by your boss*?"

So, what is wrong with coworkers praising each other? The next time your coworker does something (it does not even need to be something extraordinary), praise him/her for a job well done. The praise, to be effective, must be sincere, very specific, timely, and show an impact. For example, "Thank you for getting this report to me on time. That way, I can do my analysis and turn the report in to the boss on schedule."

Over time, you'll notice that praise becomes contagious. Suddenly, several coworkers are praising each other and morale will increase. Paula will notice this and try to find out what's going on. Tell her! By the way, don't forget to praise Paula as well. She just may see how good it makes her feel and may start doing some of it herself. Even if she doesn't, you and your coworkers will feel more gratified by giving and receiving praise in the workplace.

Another proactive strategy to force communication with Paula is to set up regularly scheduled meetings with her. Depending on your job and the need for communication, the meetings might be once a day for five minutes, or possibly once a week for 15 minutes. Either way, the purpose is to set a structured environment that forces this bad boss to communicate with you and increase your rate of survival!

In Closing...

By the way, there are some advantages to having a bad boss. You can study his/her style and, when management opportunities come to you, you will know how *not* to manage others. Also, having a bad boss will help you really appreciate all the good bosses out there!

Finally, life would be much easier if all bad bosses fit neatly into one of these five categories. Unfortunately, they do not. You may have a boss that is part two-faced, part poor communicator and two parts tyrant. So, you will need to combine some of these strategies to get started. Even if you implement these techniques and use them repeatedly, the boss may never change. However, your chances of surviving him or her will!

Try this:

Pick just one strategy from this chapter and try to use it with your bad boss over the next 21 days.

Strategy:

Start date:

End date:

Number of times used (approximate):

"OK, it's really not like *stealing* from the company. It's more like *borrowing* the money for a really, really long time!"

These strategies will seem like "common sense." However, they are definitely not commonly practiced. Most people believe that they adhere to these principles, but many do not.

Chapter 6 Stepping Forward as an Ethical Leader... in 8 minutes *or less*

All employees are leaders—potentially. A leader does not necessarily have to be a manager. Simply defined, a leader is someone with one or more followers. Almost everyone's actions in the workplace are followed by at least one other person a minimum of one time. Therefore, whether you realize it or not, there are times when you are a leader in the workplace.

So, what is an "ethical" leader, and why is it so important to be seen as one?

Think about a time in your career when someone said or did something that struck you the wrong way. It just felt wrong. You probably didn't think about it in terms of whether it was ethical or not; you just knew it wasn't right.

That feeling that you had is what this chapter is all about. In the simplest of terms, being "ethical" means consistently doing the right thing.

Consider the following example:

> You are a salesperson for Boogie Woogie Music Unlimited. You supply disco music to nightclubs around the country.
>
> For the last several years, you have struggled to find enough buyers of disco music to achieve your sales quotas. You have been working very hard and you believe your company has set your sales quotas too high.
>
> In order to meet your sales goals and keep your job, you have been going door-to-door to small, lesser-known clubs such as The Freak Out Spout, The Disco Mix-o and The White Shoes Moves.
>
> Your family is tired of living paycheck to paycheck, and it looks as though you are going to have to give up your long-time career of selling disco music when you suddenly get a break.
>
> The largest bar in the area, The Bar, is converting to a disco format, and they'll need lots of disco music. If you can convince them to buy at least 1,000 CDs,

you will get a 35% commission. If they order less than 1,000, you get a 15% commission.

Despite your best efforts, the final order was for 975 CDs. However, someone in your accounting office made an error. The CD "Johnny T's Top 50 Disco Hits" was billed out 50 times, instead of once. Your accounting office did not catch the error, nor did The Bar, as they have just paid their invoice.

The only reason that you found out is that your commission check was a lot larger than you were expecting. When you researched it, you discovered that The Bar paid for more music than they had received and your company paid you more in commission than they were supposed to. In fact, even with the extra sales, your company's gross profit on the entire deal was lower at 1025 CDs than at 975 CDs, due to the increased commission.

Your family, on the other hand, is ecstatic about all the extra money, as the check has already hit your account via direct deposit.

So, what do you do?

The remainder of this chapter is designed to help you navigate through an ethical decision just like this one.

Follow the Right P.A.T.H.

These strategies will seem like "common sense." However, they are definitely not commonly practiced. Most people believe that they adhere to these principles, but many do not. Keep this in mind as you face tough decisions in the workplace and, chances are, you will be seen as an ethical leader:

<u>P</u>ractice what you preach
<u>A</u>nswer why
<u>T</u>ell no lie
<u>H</u>elp others

<u>Practice what you preach</u>

This is a saying that has been often quoted over the years, and it is a good principle for an ethical leader to follow.

Practice what you preach means doing what you say others should do and saying things you claim others should say in given circumstances.

The polar opposite of this is, "Do as I say, not as I do." We see this often in organizations. How do you view people who say one thing and then do another? Not credible, right? Possibly not ethical either!

Once you have set a standard verbally for how others should act or what others should do, it is important for you to do the same or reestablish the standard with those you communicated with initially.

For example, let's say that one of your coworkers is speaking negatively about someone who is not around to defend himself. You think that is wrong, and you state, "We shouldn't be talking about him behind his back. We should give him the opportunity to respond in person."

This is a *great* response in this situation. If you look at gossip and rumors in the workplace, the main reason why they exist and have a dramatic effect on people is that *we tend to listen to the rumor or gossip* rather than stopping it by saying, "Let's go get the person we are talking about and give him an opportunity to hear what's being said."

But, *noooooooooooooooo*. We feel some sort of need to be curious. So, we allow the conversation to continue. In other words, it is the fault of the person listening to the rumor, because if the listener refuses to continue listening, then the rumor cannot be spread.

Bottom line: If you make a statement against talking about someone behind his/her back, you have to make sure that you never talk behind someone else's back.

Practice what you preach.

Answer why

This is an important part of being seen as ethical.

Unless you have a tremendous amount of charisma, you need to explain to others why you made a particular decision or acted a certain way. If others understand your motives or reasons and can put themselves in your shoes, your chances of being seen as ethical greatly increase.

On the other hand, many times people do or say things that we do not believe are ethical because we simply do not understand the logic behind it.

Here is an example:

Bosley, your boss, has just announced that you are going to need to improve your productivity by 10% beginning next month. Bosley does not give you an explanation for the increase. In fact, he says, "Just do it."

These types of decisions are made in every workplace all the time. Whether you work at a privately held company, a not-for-profit organization or a government agency, you have some type of production guidelines that must be met.

That doesn't really help you understand Bosley's decision, does it? What if Bosley did a better job of explaining the entire picture to you? What if he said something like this:

"We have reached a point where we have to make some tough decisions for our department due to financial considerations. Here are the options I was able to choose from:

1. Eliminate your position.
2. Offer you a 10% cut in pay
3. Reduce your insurance benefits
4. Eliminate your retirement plan
5. Increase your productivity by 10%, starting next month."

Which would you prefer?

When it is explained in this light, the decision becomes much easier to understand, doesn't it? Note that you may still disagree with the option Bosley chose (number five), but you can at least follow the logic and the reasons.

"Answer why" can and should be used no matter who you are communicating with in the workplace—your boss, coworkers, vendors, customers, employees, etc.

Tell no lie

There are many different degrees of lying, right? There is the white lie, where allegedly no one gets hurt. Then we have the flat out, boldface lie, which is a significant deviation from the truth. And, there are varying degrees of lies in between.

The problem is that people in the workplace perceive the various degrees of lying differently.

For some people, the white lie is just as bad as the flat out, boldface lie because it speaks of that person's overall character.

Many people believe the best predictor of the future is the past. So, while you may perceive that white lie in the workplace as no big deal, others may assume that if you lied once, you'll lie again.

Hence, tell no lie.

Too late, huh?

Building credibility in the workplace so that you are seen as ethical is definitely a work in progress. You can always start today and, assuming too much damage has not already been done, you can be seen as an ethical leader in due time. But, remember this: The climb up the ladder is long and is earned a rung at a time. The trip down is a relative freefall and can happen in the blink of an eye.

So, tell no lie!

By the way, withholding information is the same thing as lying! If you make a mistake, stand up and admit it rather than trying to cover it up or (worse yet) blaming it on someone else. Ethical people make mistakes, but they also fess up to those mistakes. To err is human; to blame others falsely or cover up is unethical!

Help others

What does helping others have to do with being ethical?

Much of the workplace attitude today seems to be built on selfishness. "I'm going to get as far as I can and to heck with everyone else!" Doesn't sound too ethical, does it?

The opposite, then, is unselfishness. You will notice that once you go out of your way to help others get what they want, they will soon (or eventually) start to help you get what you want.

You can help others by teaching or mentoring your coworkers. This will also help you because the best way to learn something and to internalize positive behaviors is to teach it to others. However, helping others in the workplace has to be completely unconditional in order for it to work. You may hope that your behavior will be reciprocated. Unfortunately, this is not always the case. Even so, others will take notice of your selfless actions.

What can you teach? All of us have special skills—things that we are better at doing than others. One of the characteristics of a great workplace is the showcase of different talents and skills that all come together, just like the ingredients of a recipe come together to make a great dish. Figure out what you add to the recipe and make it your goal to show it to others.

You can also mentor others in the workplace by taking them "under your wing." In so doing, you can help them to overcome workplace challenges that you have already met and overcome.

A final bit of advice -- when others succeed in the workplace, be happy for them and help them enjoy their successes rather than be bitter and jealous and angry that the same success did not happen to you.

So, What About Boogie Woogie?

Let's return to our dilemma at the beginning of the chapter and hear the rest of the story.

> This fictional example was largely based on a real-life workplace scenario. The salesperson in this case was faced with a tough decision involving ethics. On the one hand, she worked very hard, felt the sales goals set were unrealistic, and very much wanted to make her family happy.
>
> On the other hand, it wasn't her money!
>
> The salesperson decided to do the right thing and she informed the employer about the overpayment of the commission and the fact that the customer was overcharged.
>
> The employer, very grateful for the salesperson's honesty and ethical behavior, allowed the salesperson to keep

the commission. The employer, in an effort to be ethical, immediately issued a credit to the customer and explained what happened.

The customer, in return, not only provided the company (and the salesperson) with more business, he also referred the salesperson to other customers!

Following the Right P.A.T.H. in the workplace will earn you the respect of the other employees and will ultimately lead to your own personal satisfaction and success!

Jim was grateful to have the support of his "friends" at work when he missed a question in the "game show challenge" at the annual company picnic.

Always be aware of perceptions, as they are reality in the minds of those who have them!

Chapter 7 Managing Friendships and Relationships ... in 6 minutes *or less*

We spend about 1/3 of our lives working, so it is only natural that we will develop friendships and/or relationships at work, right?

No problem. Don't worry, be happy.

Well, this should work in theory at least. But, sometimes there is a problem that causes us to worry, and to be unhappy. Occasionally, *very unhappy.*

This chapter is primarily dedicated to preserving valuable workplace relationships and friendships. It will look at relationships between employees and managers as well as relationships between coworkers.

Employee/Manager

This is one of the most challenging relationships you can be in—whether you are the employee or the manager. In this situation, do you think it is possible that some other employees in the department are going to perceive this manager is favoring this employee because of the relationship?

Sure!

Further, is it possible that some people (including the employee/friend) will perceive that the manager is harder on this employee because the manager does not want others to think that s/he is favoring this employee?

Of course!

And, is it possible that both these scenarios could be happening within the department at the same time?

Yep!

No matter how effectively you are implementing the strategies suggested in this chapter, the *perception* of unfairness will almost always be there. Your goal, then, is to minimize it.

Some organizations have policies against fraternization (association with someone outside the workplace) and/or nepotism (employment of relatives). These policies would take precedence over any advice offered in this chapter.

One important thing to realize is the manager must hold the friend/employee as accountable for performance expectations and policy adherence as s/he would hold other employees. All too frequently, the manager makes a serious mistake by either going easy on the friend or holding the friend to a higher standard. This will inevitably lead to the negative perceptions mentioned previously.

In other words, you should not expect any special treatment if you are the employee. If the manager is holding you accountable for an expectation or policy through a performance review, disciplinary action, or verbal conversation, you should not take it personally because special treatment is expected.

For workplace friendships and relationships to be successful, you have to be willing to separate the relationship outside of work from the relationship at work.

Putting any kind of pressure on the manager during these meetings by saying something like, "Come on. You don't need to give me that written warning. I thought we were friends," will only make the situation worse.

Please keep in mind that the goal of any effective manager should be to be respected by the others, not necessarily to be liked.   The role of management is not to win a popularity contest! If the manager is respected AND liked, that's a good combination, but it is not essential for the manager to be well-liked. Here's an example:

Manny, the manager is friends outside the workplace with Lori, the employee. One day, Lori is late for work. In this situation, Manny would typically issue a written warning to the employee, because it is company policy to arrive at work on time and because it is important.

In this case, Manny does not give Lori a written warning, because that may cause her not to "like" him. When he makes that choice, it causes other employees to lose respect for Manny. Interestingly, coworkers typically lose respect for Lori, as well. This loss of respect is because they perceive "favoritism."

Now, in a perfect world, the coworkers would never find out what disciplinary action, if any, was taken with Lori. Certainly, they would never find out from Manny! However, somehow, people seem to learn what happened.

Therefore, Manny's role is to consistently hold Lori accountable, and Lori's role is to accept the fact that that is Manny's responsibility.

The other extreme is also possible; Manny may discipline Lori more harshly than her coworkers.

Not only will Lori see this as unfair, but Lori's other friends in the department may also recognize this unfair situation and lose respect for Manny as a leader.

The moral of the story is the manager must give the same treatment to all employees in similar situations. Get it? Got it? Good!

So, let's take a look at prevention. A manager and employee must be proactive when a relationship develops at work. A proactive approach is actually the best cure for reducing the likelihood that anything negative will happen in the first place.

Whether the manager or the employee is new to the department, or when the relationship has just developed between an existing manager and employee, it is important to set the "foundation structure" of the relationship. The structure should, minimally, adhere to the following rules:

1. Talk only business at work and avoid business conversations outside of work.

At times, this may seem to be unrealistic, but your ability to separate the two will greatly influence whether or not both relationships are successful. Many times, these topics are intermixed, and it becomes hard to separate the relationship at work and outside the workplace. A lighthearted approach to addressing this issue is usually more effective than an angry one.

For example, in the workplace Manny asks Lori, "So, what's for dinner tonight?" Lori's answer could be, "Is that a personal question you're asking me at work?" She could also respond by saying, "NOTHING. After that written warning you just gave me, I don't care if you eat garbage!" Which do you think would be more effective to preserve both relationships? Similarly, if Manny asks Lori a question about her job duties outside of work, she could respond by saying, "Is that a workplace question you're asking me on my time off?"

Try to keep the two situations separate as much as possible.

2.   Agree on accountability

The manager will treat the employee the same as s/he treats all other employees. If a perception ever develops that this is not the case, the employee should bring this to the attention of the manager in a way that is respectful and preserves the relationship.

The employee should make a commitment not to take it personally at work if the manager holds the employee accountable for an expectation.

3.   Avoid "public displays of affection" at work!

Not only are these displays distracting, they also tend to lead to perceptions of favoritism by others. Additionally, sexual harassment allegations could come into play if another employee observes these displays and feels it is creating a hostile work environment for him/her.

There is no need to avoid or ignore the other person, either. Just try to avoid handholding, hugging, massages, flirting, pet names—you get the picture!

4.   Make a contingency plan

What happens if the relationship ends? Most of the time, this is the BIG reason why managers and employees avoid relationships in the first place—the dread of still working together if things go sour.

Agree on a contingency plan in the very beginning. This is a tough subject because it can appear as though the person bringing it up is assuming the relationship is not going to make it. Although this can be a rough hurdle, it is generally much more uncomfortable if the relationship ends and there is no contingency plan in place.

In some cases, the agreement may be to continue a professional relationship in the workplace. In other situations, the manager or the employee may agree to seek a transfer to another department.

Here is the bottom line: Even in companies where there is no formal policy governing these types of relationships, the employer always has the right to focus on the relationship's impact in the workplace. In cases where a negative impact exists such as perceptions of unfairness, sexual harassment, low productivity, morale, attendance or other impacts, the employer may take action. It is better to avoid getting into these situations in the first place, isn't it?

Between Coworkers

Since the potential for really negative things happening in a relationship between coworkers is not as great as it is in an employee/manager relationship, this chapter devotes much less time to this type of relationship.

Nonetheless, many of the strategies outlined previously for the manager/employee relationship are also appropriate here. Discussing business at work and personal matters away from work, avoiding "public displays of affection," and deciding what to do if the relationship ends are all applicable.

It is important to note that sometimes others perceive a lack of productivity between two friends at work who chat quite a bit. This can cause animosity within the workplace if it appears to be excessive. Always be aware of perceptions, as they are reality in the minds of those who have them!

This chapter will conclude with a personal story that underscores another aspect of relationships at work.

Several years ago, two managers who worked for me informed me that they were dating. My eventual response was, "As long as it does not affect the workplace in a negative way, I am OK with it." I admit that I was not thrilled with the development at the time! However, both were professionals, and the relationship worked out. My wife and I attended their wedding a few years ago, and today they have a child. This personal experience helped reshape my viewpoint on workplace relationships forever!

Benny's coworkers were always there for him whenever he needed assistance leaving the office at the end of the day.

Leaving an industrial-size case of breath mints on Brad's desk awaiting his morning arrival to work (and his morning breath) will not cause him to have a reaction such as, "Oh, my. Look at these mints. *My breath must be offensive!*"

Chapter 8 Tackling Tough Situations, such as Body Odor... in 7 minutes *or less*

Over the years, people in the workplace have tried to avoid or handle the most difficult situations in different ways. Most times, the results are unsuccessful. Many times, the results are disastrous! In this chapter, you will be given a proven model for successfully tackling these tough situations that will give you the greatest opportunity to bring resolution to the problem once and for all.

Let's start with the things we typically and traditionally do that are not effective. We'll use your coworker, Bad Breath Brad, as our target for change. Though Brad's breath is bad, the model will work for any offensive body odor, as well as other irritating traits (such as talking too loud on the telephone, popping gum, interrupting you in the middle of a conversation, bad cell phone habits, cursing, being disrespectful...you get the picture).

These things do NOT work:

1. Jokes or sarcasm

Leaving an industrial-size case of breath mints on Brad's desk awaiting his morning arrival to work (and his morning breath) will not cause him to have a reaction such as, "Oh, my. Look at these mints. *My breath must be offensive!*" This is important to understand because Brad does not know his breath is horrid and will not get the hint. Why not? Simply because he has lived with it for so long, he does not know the difference!

This is particularly frustrating for you because you are thinking, "How could he not know?" What you need to understand is that *he doesn't!* If you started working at a paint store today, you would find the fumes to be overwhelmingly offensive. Over time, however, you would become so used to working in that environment that you would not even notice it.

Offering Brad a single mint ("Hey, Brad, would you like one of these breath mints? They're *really* good. Mmmm.") won't do the trick, either. Though you may have fixed the odor for the moment, it will soon be back in full force because you have addressed the symptom rather than the problem.

Sarcasm ("Hey, Brad. Did something crawl up inside you and die?") and jokes will not work. Brad will simply take it personally and think that you just do not like him.

2. Ignore it

"If I wait long enough, someone else will tell him, he'll figure it out on his own, or maybe he'll just quit!"

Fat chance of any of these things happening. It has not happened yet, has it?

3. Tell the boss

Guess what? The boss typically does not know how to handle it either.

4. Tell other coworkers

The passive-aggressive approach here ends up getting back to Brad, but the message is totally different than what you intended once it travels through the grapevine. Ultimately, Brad will just take it as a personal put-down and will not fix the problem. You'll be worse off than doing nothing.

Here's a model to achieve success:

Follow this plan step-by-step in the order stated. Make sure this conversation is held in private!

1. "What I am about to share with you is not easy for me."

The purpose of this opening statement is to let Brad know that you are about to tell him something difficult. This will usually ensure you have his attention.

2. "If I were you, I would want to know this. You are probably not even aware of it."

Here, you are letting Brad know the reason why you are bringing this to his attention. You are also giving him an opportunity to "save face" in this difficult scenario.

3. "I have noticed..."

The classic mistake that many people make here is to say, "It has been brought to my attention", or, "One of your coworkers told me that...". There will be a place for that later. For now, it is important for Brad to know this is *your* observation and feedback.

4. "...an odor coming from your breath."

It is important to be direct here. Avoid saying, " I have noticed a hygiene concern", for example. Also avoid, "Your breath stinks!" There is a way to be direct, yet tactful, so that Brad does not take it personally.

5. "Other coworkers and customers have also mentioned this to me."

Now that you have taken responsibility for your statement, and you have been direct, you can validate it to show Brad that you are not the only one who feels this way.

6. "It is offensive to them, and it is causing some of our customers to take their business elsewhere."

It is very important that Brad clearly understands the IMPACT of his bad breath on you, other coworkers, customers, productivity, morale, or whatever it is affecting. In the event that whatever Brad is doing does not have an impact on the workplace, don't make an issue of it! This part is important, since he does not notice his bad breath. He will usually think, "So what. That's your problem, not mine." It is vital to begin to get "buy in" from him that a problem really exists.

7. "Can you see how important it is to try and remedy this situation?"

This statement, coupled with a "Yes" from Brad, seals the buy-in. If he says "No" or wavers, then go back to steps 5 and 6 and show him a different angle.

8. "Do you have any ideas on a possible solution?"

Now that you have buy-in (very important), it is time to solve the problem for good. At this point, it is possible that Brad may say, "I have a medical problem and the Doctor is working with me to try and fix it." Or, he may say, "Maybe I will try some mouthwash or breath mints." He may also say, "I have no idea. I brush my teeth after every meal."

If Brad does not have an acceptable solution, you have to take the initiative by making some recommendations. Personal experiences seem to work the best here. For example, "I carry a trial-sized mouthwash, and I use it after every time I eat something. I also carry these breath mints and I eat one about every hour or two. Perhaps you could try that."

Whether you come up with a solution or Brad does, the important thing is that he agrees to implement it.

   9. "I'm glad you have committed to using mouthwash in the morning as well as after you eat something. I'll let you know if this is making a difference. Thank you for listening."

Reaffirm expectations, indicate you will be doing a follow-up of some kind, and sincerely thank Brad for helping you handle such a tough situation.

Other Applications

This model will help you address and resolve virtually any tough situation in the workplace. Let's say one of your coworkers, Speakerphone Sally, likes to talk to everyone via, you guessed it, a speakerphone. This is annoying to you, because it is hard for you to concentrate on what you are doing with her entire conversation booming all over the workplace like a rock concert!

Once again, the traditional ways of dealing with this problem are not effective. Ignoring it, using sarcasm, complaining to others and going to the boss usually do not work. Let's see how this one might play out, assuming Sally plays "hard ball."

You: "Sally, what I am about to share with you is uncomfortable for me, and, if I were you, I would appreciate someone bringing it to my attention."

Sally: "Yeah? What is it this time?"

You: "Well, you may not even be aware of this. I have noticed that you talk to others quite often using your speakerphone. Your coworkers have noticed it as well. It is distracting for me when I am trying to concentrate on a report or when I am trying to speak to someone on the phone."

Sally: (Silence)

You: "Can you see how this would be very distracting?"

Sally: "I am very busy doing all the work around here. I talk on the speakerphone so that I can get all the reports I need in front of me while the person on the other line is telling me what they need. Holding the phone in between my ear and shoulder hurts my neck."

You: "I can definitely appreciate that pain. I felt the same way, and I ended up getting a hands-free headset so that I could be freed up to pull reports and talk on the phone at the same time."

Sally: "Well, good for you."

You: "I have also talked to some of your customers and they have indicated that they are frustrated when you talk to them using the speakerphone because your voice cuts out many times. That's why they ask you to repeat what you've told them quite often."

Sally: "Yeah, that does happen."

You: "So, what do you think would be a good solution here?"

Sally: "Well, I guess I could try the hands free set."

You: "Thanks for your understanding, and for committing to the hands free set, rather than the speakerphone. I'll let you know if it makes a difference."

In closing...

You can use this model whether you are talking to a coworker, an employee, a boss, a customer, a vendor, or even someone in your personal life. Because this approach is assertive, you will find that very few people are offended by it. In the rare case that someone does not appreciate the way you tackled the tough situation, it will at least plant a seed in his/her mind.

If you try this plan, and it is unsuccessful, go back and make sure you addressed all nine points of the model. The order of the points is also significant. Chances are, you may have omitted one or more points or changed the sequential order. Also, since you will likely not have this book in front of you when you address the concern, it is best to practice your technique with a friend or family member playing the role of the annoying coworker. Here's a template to get you started:

First person you want to address (initials):

Irritating habit/difficult situation:

Today's date:

Deadline to address it:

Second person you want to address (initials):

Irritating habit/difficult situation:

Today's date:

Deadline to address it:

On the day that Betty was asked to add filing to her growing list of responsibilities, she enrolled in a class to learn how to work using her feet as well!

It is important to note that, contrary to popular belief, companies do not institute changes just to make employees' lives miserable. There is usually a very good reason behind the change.

Chapter 9 Thriving Amidst Change...in 10 minutes *or less*

Got change? Not the kind that jingles in your pocket, but the kind that shakes...as in shakes up you and/or your team at work.

Change is not easy, and this book does not pretend to claim that it is. Change puts us all out of our "comfort zone" that we are accustomed to. Change, however, is growth. And, growth is a part of life. Therefore, change is a part of life. In this chapter, the focus will be on dealing with change, and it will look at several different angles, approaches and strategies for handling it when it happens (and it *will* happen in your workplace, perhaps before you are done reading this book!).

The Magic Formula

O + R = O/R

Occurrence + Reaction = Outcome/Result

The occurrence is something that happens in the workplace that you may have absolutely no control over. Your reaction, however, is always something that you have full control over. It is your reaction to the occurrence that will determine the outcome/result.

Consider this example:

> A major Fortune 500 company hired me for a series of speaking engagements. They wanted me to talk to their employees about learning valuable workplace skills. That part was not unusual.
>
> The unusual part was that this company was going to lay off an entire division of their company, and I was being hired to speak to these employees who did not know if they were going to have a job for another two hours, two days, two months or two years.
>
> Now, that's change and unpredictability.
>
> As I was preparing the various topics this company wanted me to speak on, I was also preparing myself to face a bitter, hostile audience. After all, several of

these folks had worked for this company for an average of 15-25 years and had always envisioned retiring with this company.

It was an unforeseeable downturn in a particular segment of the economy as a result of the 9-11 tragedy that made it necessary for this division to close. In other words, it was not the fault of anyone working for this company and was completely out of their control.

So, I was expecting the worst reaction of bitterness and I expected to have many "prisoners" ("I do not want to be here") in the audience.

What I got was the complete opposite. These folks believed in the O + R = O/R formula. They knew they had no control over the occurrence (the layoffs) nor did they know if they would have their jobs for a matter of days, months or years. But, they knew that they needed to have the tools to go out and get another job, and they realized their reaction to the occurrence would ultimately determine their future.

So, they set out to learn. Many talked about starting a new career, a new hobby, or even self-employment. Some set goals to return to school and finish their education. Others discussed possibly spending more time with their family as they were searching for a new job.

> But almost all stayed committed to excelling at their current job with their current company. It turned out that those who chose this path were retained for several years and those who did not were some of the first to get laid off.
>
> O + R = O/R

You can probably think of several changes that happened in your life that were not positive at first, but you chose to see a different side of things and changed the outcome.

Christopher Reeve is a great example of this. How can you go from being Superman to being incapable of self-care in an instant? What a change!

However, Reeve understood O + R = O/R. Rather than feel sorry for himself and focus on all the things he could no longer do, he chose to accept the change and focus on the many things he could still do. To this day, he has tremendously helped many others who are in a similar condition.

Now, think of the changes that happen in your workplace. Chances are they are not as dramatic as what happened to the Fortune 500 Company or to Christopher Reeve. One thing, however, is true about change—it probably seems a lot worse today than it will in the future when you are able to put it into perspective.

The Lighter Side of Change

Change is growth, and growth is a constant part of life. Therefore, change is a normal part of life. There have been numerous changes over the course of history that probably seemed painful or odd at the time but that we appreciate today. Let's look at a few of these!

<u>Pen and Paper</u>

Imagine if these modern marvels had not come along! Before pen and paper, we had stone tablets and a chisel. Therefore, this book would weigh about 500 lbs! If you wanted to take a copy of it to work, you would need a very strong wheelbarrow (assuming the wheel has been invented) and some very strong friends to help you wheel it!

The idea of changing to pen and paper must have been ridiculous way back when. Why change something that was working perfectly well at the time?

Fortunately, this change did take place. Can you imagine signing for a home mortgage without pen and paper? If you think a lot of work goes into it today, imagine if the entire transaction was carved in stone! Just getting through the disclosures would be exhausting! And, since there was no way to make copies, think how long it would take the bank to draw up all the "paperwork" (or "tablet work" in this case). You would need to decide on the house you are going to live in by age

12, just so that the paperwork would be ready for you to move in at age 25. Hopefully, whoever is living with you will like the house!

Yes, we complain a lot about "all the paperwork" in the workplace, but it would be a lot worse if it weren't for that change!

Clothes

Good thing the fig leaf and loincloth were changed! Many of you complain about the clothing coworkers wear in the office every day. We frequently hear comment such as:

"Does he *know* that tie and suit do not go together?"

"Where did she get that *awful* dress? The reject pile?"

"Those pants went out of style twenty years ago—just like his haircut."

"Can you believe she is wearing *that*? She must have spent all morning painting it on!"

Yep, if you struggle with what your coworkers are wearing now, imagine them with practically nothing on.

Then again, don't.

<u>Personal Toiletries</u>

Many people are glad certain personal things were invented over time. Deodorant is one that comes to mind. Of course, some coworkers still do not seem to believe in using it (refer back to chapter 8). But imagine a world with no deodorant. Better yet, how odd must it have been way back when the "deodorant pioneers" started wearing it?

Can you imagine the dialogue?

"What's that AWFUL smell?"

"That's John. He calls it 'deodorant'."

"That stuff STINKS!"

Ditto with cologne, perfume, mouthwash, toothpaste, soap, and all those other things that we consider necessities. In fact, some hotel chains make a promise to their guests to keep such toiletries on hand "just in case" guests forgot something! Why? Because we cannot imagine living without these things for even a day now! What a change!

And the grandest change of them all...imagine a world with NO MAKEUP! How odd it must have been for the first people to wear makeup! Imagine the ridicule those folks must have taken from those around them.

Physical Appearance

Change is growth, and growth is life. But, what if we never changed and we never grew? What if our physical appearance and mannerisms were exactly the same as when we were born? Well, then we would be working around a bunch of crying, whining babies in need of constant attention and incapable of doing anything by themselves. Wait...some workplaces are *still* like that, anyway! See chapter 1 for more assistance!

Enough Humor—GWTF

OK, so the humor strategy does not work for everyone. The next tool is something that you can use in the workplace to help either yourself or coworkers deal more effectively with change—GWTF!

Or, Go With The Flow!

> Credit for GWTF has to be given to my wife, Yvette. In fact, she uses the phrase on me several times in a given month! After years of absorbing it, I think I have finally understood its meaning.

Imagine your workplace as a river flowing with a fairly strong current at some times, and at other times it is very still—almost like a lake. When the storms come along (and sometimes they can be severe, even to include flooding the river) the surge is quite forceful. The "storm" represents change in the workplace and the current is the ensuing result.

In the workplace, many of us spend all our energy fighting the current to stay where we are. Think about all the energy, time and effort required just battling the raging rapids. We look to grab on to *anything*—a tree limb, a rock, an anchored coworker—*anything* to avoid being swept down the river.

After days of doing this, how do we feel? Physically and mentally exhausted. And, if the current is able to force us down the river a little, what do we typically do that makes it much worse? That's right, we actually attempt to swim back upstream to get back to where we were before!

So, once the storm is over, if we have been successful at holding our ground, we find that we are exhausted and probably alone on the river!

The next time there is a storm, GWTF. Let the current take you down the river. Get in the boat and enjoy the power of the rapids and the fun experience as the white water whisks you along.

For those of you who are white water rapids enthusiasts, it is a lot more fun on class 4 or 5 rapids than it is paddling on still waters, isn't it? Sure, still waters are OK every now and then to admire the beauty of the scenery and to rest your body, but you cannot wait to get to the real thing.

Your heart is beating faster at the prospect of the gushing rapids up ahead!

This is what successful people in the workplace do. The next time you or a coworker is having trouble with a change, just say, "GWTF!"

If you GWTF, then TGIF will not seem that far away!

> As a manager, I practiced GWTF as I told the companies I worked for that they could transfer me to any place in the US at any time with any notice. My "record move" was when the company called me at 5pm one day at work and asked me to get on a plane the next morning.
>
> In this true story, I had a little more advanced notice (not much, though). A company I worked for (Marriott Corporation-great company) asked me to move to Minneapolis, MN.
>
> The first thing I did was to get a map to see where in Minnesota Minneapolis actually was located. The next thing I did was to look up the average winter temperature (80 degrees below zero), the average length of winter (10 ½ months) and the average monthly snowfall (50 feet per month). Well, it wasn't *that* bad, but over the years the story gets embellished, kind of like the 9-inch fish that becomes 6 feet long over time.

Let's just say I was not excited to be
going!

It turns out that I spent two years there,
and they were two wonderful years. The
Minnesotans were unbelievably friendly (I
have good friends there to this day), the
quality of life was outstanding, and the
weather was, well, just about as bad as I
had imagined it would be!

An added bonus for me as an avid sports
fan was that during the two years I was
there, Minneapolis hosted the Super
Bowl, Stanley Cup Finals, NCAA
Basketball Final Four, World Series, US
Open (Golf) and the Special Olympics.

Minnesota was the last place I would
have chosen to live, and I was not happy
about the change at the time. Eventually,
I learned GWTF and, even to this day, I
get very excited when I book a speaking
engagement in the Twin Cities (yes, even
in the winter!).

Seeing the Positive Side of Change

Most change has two sides—a positive (the
Minnesota people, quality of life and sports) and
negative (the winters). Which side do you choose
to see?

Consider the cost of goods and services you
purchase today versus the prices in the 1930's.

Wool sweaters were about $0.95, as were table lamps. A gas stove would run you about $18.50 and an electric washing machine would set you back less than $35! Too bad those prices had to change, isn't it?

Not really! Take a look at wages in the 1930's. If you worked in a factory or as a cook, you would make about $16. Accountants and Doctors were paid around $40 and $58, respectively. By the way, those wages are *per week*! Thankfully, wages have changed over the years as well.

Find the positives in any change (sometimes you have to look harder than others) and avoid dwelling on the negative.

Why?

Sometimes, it helps to seek out the reason for the change. It is important to note that, contrary to popular belief, companies do not institute changes just to make employees' lives miserable. There is usually a very good reason behind the change.

If you are the one making the change that will affect others, explain WHY you are making the change and try to show the benefits of that change. You'll find that people are more receptive to it when they know the reason behind it.

Everything Happens for a Reason

The final strategy in thriving on change is to realize that everything happens for a reason (credit to my mother for drilling this into my head). At the time, the change seems painful, and there does not seem to be a logical explanation for it.

However, over time, most of you will be able to see where the change fit in your career or life and why it had to happen that way. Just keep in mind that change gives you an opportunity to grow.

Bill's coworkers weren't quite so happy about the way that he had decided to "apply himself" and try to climb to the top!

If you talk to successful people in the workplace, very few will say they achieved success by luck or chance. Very few inherited success. The majority of successful people are that way because they had a dream and turned that dream into a reality.

Chapter 10 Setting Goals and Motivating Yourself...in 5 minutes *or less*

How are you going to get to where you want to go if you do not know how or when you are going to get there?

Let's say you are in Asheville, North Carolina. You are given a car and the keys, and are instructed, "Drive this car to Boise, Idaho." Would you just get in the car and start driving?

Probably not. Unless you know the best route from Asheville to Boise, you would probably get lost frequently along the way. You may take five times as long to get there because you do not know the most direct route. Some of you might not even make it there—ever!

Most people would get a map or look up step-by-step driving directions on the Internet. Some would ask directions of someone who had made the drive before. However, very few of you would just get in your car and start driving. It does not make sense!

Nevertheless, most people navigate their career just like driving to Boise without directions! They start the job without a clear vision of where they want to go or how they want to get there, and find themselves at the end of their career, wondering why they do not have the retirement money they wanted or did not attain the positions they thought they had earned in their career.

This chapter will help you set a blueprint for success if you are willing to follow it. In other words, it will help you create the map.

Setting Goals

First of all, setting goals and motivating yourself start with having a vision. Where do you want to be? If you talk to successful people in the workplace, very few will say they achieved success by luck or chance. Very few inherited success. The majority of successful people are that way because they had a dream and turned that dream into a reality.

Successful people write their goals down on paper and constantly keep these goals in front of them. So, as a first step, write down your goals and then tape the goals to your computer, post them in your workstation, hang them from your locker, or write them on the cover of your daily planner. Keep them in front of you at all times.

Next, make sure you really set GOALS, as outlined below:

Go for it. Set goals that are somewhat of a stretch but are achievable. Dare to dream. There's no feeling quite like attaining a tough goal that you set for yourself. Really think about what it is you want to achieve in life.

Outline steps. Achieving goals means setting steps (or mini goals) along the way to keep things from becoming overwhelming tasks. Make sure you have a concrete way to measure whether or not you have achieved these goals.

Act now. Set the goals today! The more time that elapses between now and when you set the goal means the goal is that much further away. Use the template at the end of this chapter to get started.

Let others know. Involve people in your "support group" by telling them what your goals are and ask them to hold you accountable for them. Your "support group" can include coworkers, your boss, friends and family. Show them your goals in writing and ask for their input. Surround yourself with people who are optimistic and think that you can do it. Avoid sharing your goals with those who are generally pessimistic.

Set specific timeframes. When you go on a trip in a car, you determine how long it will take to get there based on the mileage, road conditions, construction, traffic, how fast (or slow!) you drive, etc. For each goal, determine how long it will likely take to get there. Sometimes goals and timeframes need to be revised due to unforeseen circumstances. That's OK! Revise the date or goal and move forward!

So go for it, outline steps, act now, let others know, and set specific timeframes.

Motivation

The best way to achieve a goal is to have a "pot of gold at the end of the rainbow." The goals just mentioned represent the "rainbow" or path. Next, let's work on the gold.

Reading this book is the easy part. The reason why the title starts with "88 minutes *or less*" is because most people would not get motivated to read it if it was 500 pages long.

As you read through each chapter, you are provided with common sense strategies. If you implement them, they will likely work for you, just as they have worked for countless others in the workplace.

The one thing this book will not do for you is implement the plan. That part is up to you.

Think about your last day of work before you take a one-week vacation. Many of you need to look up the word "vacation" in the dictionary before answering the question (see chapter 12)! If you are like most people, you are able to get an incredible amount of work done on that final day before you leave. Have you ever wondered WHY?

Perhaps you did not want to come back to a pile of work (or you wanted a smaller pile). Maybe you wanted to lessen the chance you would be contacted on your vacation. Possibly guilt of having someone else do the work in your absence motivated your actions.

Whatever the reason was, you were *motivated!*

And, chances are you did not have to expend any more time or energy than a typical day. You just were more organized or more aware of the priorities set for the day. Imagine if you could be that productive every day!

You probably could if you were properly motivated!

The problem with motivation is that most employees think this is the job of their manager and wait around (sometimes for an entire career) for "someone" to motivate them!

Well, your manager probably did not "motivate" you to take a vacation; you probably decided that all on your own. Why can't it work that way all the time?

It CAN...and for people who are highly successful in the workplace, it **does!**

Look at the goals you are setting and decide what appropriate motivation needs to be added in order to make each one a goal worth achieving.

In other words, *reward yourself.* Rewards could range from relaxing on a Saturday to seeing a movie you are interested in, from going to a sporting event to reading a good book, from going out to dinner to taking a vacation, from making a home improvement to getting a massage, from buying a car to eating a candy bar. Anything that you enjoy can be a motivator!

The Template

Set a goal for yourself:

Go for it. What is the goal?

Outline steps. Set mini-goals to achieve the main goal.

Act now. Photocopy this goal and keep it in front of you.

Let others know. List a minimum of three people you will give a copy of this goal to:

Set specific timeframes. When will the goal (and mini-goals) be completed?

When this goal is achieved, I will reward myself by:

"Hi. I'm from the IRS, and I am here to help you."

You've noticed how most hotels do not have a "13th Floor" haven't you? Well, this book does not have a Chapter 11.

Chapter 11 Read and Use this Book to Avoid Chapter 11

When Susie's boss caught her daydreaming about a holiday in paradise while at her desk, he charged her with a vacation day.

When you are happy with your life in and outside of the workplace and you genuinely look forward to both, you have achieved success.

Chapter 12 Achieving Balance In and Outside the Workplace...in 5 minutes *or less*

Workaholics, this chapter is for you. It is also for just about everyone else out there. It's the last chapter in the book for the same reason that we eat dessert last in a meal—because it's the best, and it's the taste we want our mouths to remember.

How will people remember you?

Imagine you are at your own funeral. A bit morbid, admittedly, but try it. You are lying there and your friends and family are gathered around talking about you. Imagine they are saying good, positive things!

At this point, perhaps you look back on your life (maybe not literally, but...work with me here...).

Will you look back on your life and say to yourself, "I wish I had just worked about five hours per week *more*?"

NO WAY!

Rather, you will be thinking to yourself, "I wish I had spent more time with my friends and/or family, doing the things I really enjoyed."

The GOOD NEWS is that you are not at that final point yet, and you have the chance to make changes, starting now.

Work Fewer Hours and Produce More (?)

For many years, I worked an *average* of a little over 80 hours per week. My personal "record" was 119 hours...in one week. And I was proud of it.

I was told that the way to get promoted was to work all these crazy hours, and I would be rewarded.

And I was rewarded with more responsibilities and more money. When I reached the point in my career that I wanted to achieve, I realized the great cost I had paid to achieve it. Ruined relationships. Lack of sleep. Poor quality of life. Health issues. Yes, I had been "rewarded" with all of these. Something interesting happened along the way. I realized that, although I was working a lot of hours, my productivity was far less than it could have been, because of all the "rewards" described in the paragraph above.

Since then, I have been on sort of a "crusade" to help people understand that the best way to have a happy and productive work life and career is to actually achieve a balance between work and home. Countless employees have listened to me, thinking it would not work. Those same skeptical people end up coming back to me months (or years) later, thanking me for helping them achieve balance.

They tell me they are much happier at work and are much more productive. Their families and friends are also grateful to see them more often. Well, MOST are grateful!

Make a commitment to reduce your time at work by 15 minutes per week. That's only three minutes per five-day workweek, but it is a start. For those of you who are salaried, repeat this every month, or so. Over a period of time, you will notice a difference.

Employers are happy to see this happen, because you are more productive and the work environment is more positive.

A challenge here is when a boss (such as *your* boss) is working an excessive number of hours. Most employees then feel compelled to work 10 minutes per day more than the boss (come in five minutes before and leave five minutes after). This book has shown you how to model behaviors for others above you, below you and beside you to follow. Try it and see what happens. Or, you could wait for the boss to reduce his/her hours...

Having Fun at Work

The best employers realize that happy employees are the key to happy customers and a positive work environment. And, where there is a positive work environment, people tend to be happier at home, because they tend not to bring work problems home. In other words, it becomes a self-perpetuating positive cycle.

The Marriott Corporation does an excellent job of this. Most people think of Marriott as 100% customer-focused. They are. However, customers are not their number one priority! Their associates ("employees") are! Their philosophy is to take care of their associates and their associates will take care of their customers.

You know what? IT WORKS!

There are many examples of other companies that share this same belief. CarQuest (auto parts), Starbucks (coffee) and Southwest (airlines) are just a few.

Have you ever noticed how much fun the employees who work at Southwest Airlines are having? Do all employees of all airlines appear to be having that much fun? What is it about Southwest? Many people credit the CEO. The reality is that all employees have to be committed to having fun in order for it to work.

Having fun at work has to start somewhere. If you are not fortunate enough to work for a company like Marriott, CarQuest, Starbucks, Southwest or one of the others with this type of workplace philosophy, what can you do?

Start having fun!

People really would prefer to have fun in the workplace, rather than be miserable. In some organizations, however, misery dominates. So, who will dare to be different?

Why not you?

Get together with some of your coworkers, and make a pact to make the workplace a "funplace." Gather ideas. Have a joke of the day or quote of the day. Start a contest. Make sure you are not violating any company policy. People will catch on, and they'll want to join in.

Helping Others

One of the best ways you can feel better about where you work is to help someone else who is struggling.   Give someone a copy of this book. Share with them what has worked for you.

If you commit to helping others in the workplace, you will be surprised how many people will reciprocate and help you when you least expect it. Make your help unconditional, and watch what happens.   Learning to be genuinely happy for others' successes is a much more important trait than focusing on your own successes.

When is Success Achieved?

When you are happy with your life in and outside of the workplace and you genuinely look forward to both, you have achieved success.

Sometimes, staying on top of the mountain is tougher than the climb itself.   The enemy of success is complacency. So, be happy where you are, and look to achieve greater success in and outside the workplace.   Perhaps you have now reached your "dream job." Great! Keep working at it to make it even better than before.

Successful people in the workplace never give up. They look for ways around obstacles, they move the barriers, or they take a different path. Successful people appreciate what they have, but they strive for more.   They are always thinking and coming up with ideas, even though most of their ideas are not implemented or given a second thought. Successful people approach challenges head-on   and   assertively   handle   bosses, coworkers, customers and business partners in a way that earns them respect again and again.

Successful people set goals and are able to motivate themselves to achieve them. They dare to dream, knowing that all dreams do not come true, but also knowing that working without dreaming is a nightmare.

Dream it. Try it. Do it right. Do it well. Do it *now!*